Popular Girls

Etiquette Diary

TEEN LEADERSHIP EDITION

by

Wilvena McDowell

authorHOUSE®

AuthorHouse™
1663 Liberty Drive
Bloomington, IN 47403
www.authorhouse.com
Phone: 1-800-839-8640

Published by AuthorHouse 5/22/2012

ISBN: 978-1-4685-9467-6 (sc)
ISBN: 978-1-4685-9466-9 (e)

AuthorHouse™
1663 Liberty Drive
Bloomington, IN 47403
www.authorhouse.com
Phone: 1-800-839-8640

Published by AuthorHouse 5/22/2012

ISBN: 978-1-4685-9467-6 (sc)
ISBN: 978-1-4685-9466-9 (e)

Popular Girls
Etiquette Diary

TEEN LEADERSHIP EDITION

by
Wilvena McDowell

authorHOUSE®

You define what being Popular is!

Table of Contents

Chapter 1: What Makes a Girl Popular?

Chapter 2: Posture & Poise

Chapter 3: Gossip Girls Etiquette

Chapter 4: Clothing Personality

Chapter 5: Conversational Etiquette

Popular Girl's Etiquette Cheat Sheet

Conclusion

Chapter 1: What Makes a Girl Popular?

What makes a young girl popular is first understanding that being popular is defined by the inner beauty of her personality and character. It is a fact that popular girls don't try to prove themselves to anyone, and are confident with who they are.

A girl's teenage years is an uncomfortable stage between childhood and adulthood. Young ladies need manners as social tools to show their level of maturity into adulthood, as well as, navigate their way through the many social events they will encounter as they grow up.

Popular Girls Etiquette Diary, was created so that every girl who feels pressured to "look perfect" can learn, step by step, how to reshape her image into the graceful young lady she has always aspired to be.

In this book, being popular has everything to do with confidence! The popular secrets girls admire in women, yet seem unable to fully grasp for themselves, are now available within the pages of this workbook. Popular Girls Etiquette is the signature guide for ladies to become more graceful, polished and classy at school, home, and everywhere they go!

You define what being Popular is!

Find out your "It Factor" and what makes your Personality shine!

Have you ever asked yourself: "Why does it seem like my friends are more popular, smarter and better looking than me?

The reason is simple: **they're not.** They just have what's called the *"It-Factor"* whereby their personality and charisma are able to charm and attract people to them in a positive way.

As of today, you can find out what character highlights work for your individual body chemistry! You too can have the *"It-Factor"* that allows your personality to shine! Once you do that you can stop feeling like everyone is more popular, smarter and better than you, and begin to realize that YOU are popular, smart and good-looking!

STEP #1

The first step in creating your popularity blueprint is finding out which character highlights will enhance your overall image. Answer the simple questionnaire on the next pages to find out what your unique character style is and what you should be doing in order for your *"It-Factor"* to shine!

If you are anxious to get started right away, turn the page! Even if all you do is read the Popular Girls Etiquette Cheat Sheet (located at the end of the workbook) you will see dramatic results in just your first few days of reading this! Then you can come back and use the rest of the book to find out what makes YOU Popular!

Identify Your Popular Personality Type

First answer this simple questionnaire to help determine how your character traits work and how your personality responds to your body chemistry!

Put a check beside all comments that accurately describes you.

1. ☐ I like to go in my closet and create new fashion outfits.

2. ☐ I like to shop at the mall all the time for the latest fashion trends.

3. ☐ I tend to dress based on how I feel, and fix my hair how I want to.

4. ☐ I tend to dress and wear my hair based on the latest style. (what the celebrities have on)

5. ☐ I usually speak in a soft, delicate voice. I've been told I need to speak up more.

6. ☐ I usually talk in a firm, direct manner. That's the only time people hear me.

7. ☐ I can be bossy and controlling and get jealous over who people get involved with.

8. ☐ I'm very confident and like getting to know people. I'm not insecure if they look prettier or are more popular than me.

9. ☐ I like to make a classy entrance and wait for others to recognize me.

10. ☐ I like to make a sophisticated entrance & introduce myself properly at social functions.

11. ☐ I like all eyes on me, so I usually like to shop or go to the nail/hair salon by myself.

12. ☐ I prefer to go to the mall, movies and nail/hair salon with my friends and family. People always look at us wherever we go because we are the center of attention.

13. ☐ I have trouble with my weight, and try to eat healthy.

14. ☐ I take pride in my appearance. I'm not concerned about how much I weigh.

15. ☐ I exercise regularly and play sports/ cheerlead/dance/ march in the band, etc.

16. ☐ When I'm around people I tend to eat more to put myself at ease if others are eating.

17. ☐ When confronted with change/something I don't want to do, I respond in a calm manner.

18. ☐ I don't like change, so in a loud voice I let people know my opinion.

19. ☐ I mainly focus on my appearance and how to enhance it. People look to me for style tips.

20. ☐ I focus on people's appearance and offer fashion advice to make them look better.

21. ☐ I take time to make decisions and react in a mature, sophisticated manner.

22. ☐ When making decisions, I tend to react quickly to get things moving. I'm a Diva!

23. ☐ I recently discussed with my friends the environment/ politics/ religion/ going to college.

24. ☐ I recently discussed with my friends school gossip/relationship drama/ and fine guys.

25. ☐ If I had to describe myself as pretty or average, I'd say I'm average.

26. ☐ If I had to describe myself as pretty or average, I'd say I'm pretty.

27. ☐ People say I'm the life of the party because I make them feel comfortable around me.

28. ☐ People say I'm the center of attention. When I walk into the room, all eyes are on me.

29. ☐ I feel true ladies should keep their thoughts to themselves unless asked to speak.

30. ☐ I feel true ladies express their ideas openly in a mature and sophisticated manner.

31. ☐ I feel true ladies should always have their hair & nails done, their clothes are pressed and clean and their manners are always graceful and elegant in public.

32. ☐ I feel true ladies should behave in a graceful manner, regardless how other's around them are acting. True ladies are respectful to everyone around them, even if they like the person or not.

33. ☐ I smirk and use intimidating facial expressions to let people know I disagree and don't understand what they're saying.

34. ☐ I use friendly gestures to let people know I'm listening to them, even if I don't fully understand or agree.

Turn the page to total your results!

Now, total your answers to identify your unique Personality Style Type. Circle the number below of each corresponding question you checked in the questionnaire. For example, if you checked #11 in the questionnaire, you would circle #11 in column 5.

1	2	3	4	5	6
1	2	3	4	5	6
7	8	9	10	11	12
13	14	15	16	17	18
19	20	21	22	23	24
25	26	27	28	29	30
31	32	33	34		
total	total	total	total	total	total

Calculate your Unique Personality Style Type:

Now count the number of circles in each column and write the total in the spaces at the bottom of the columns. **Continue Here:** First, look at Columns 1 through 4 and determine which of those columns have the most circles. Example if the total circles in *Column 1* is 7 and the total of *Column 2* is 5 then your primary number is 1, because you had more circles in column 1. Write your primary number in the box.

Primary Number

If you have the same number in more than one column, your primary number is 1. However go back and make sure you answered each question that applies to you for an accurate count.

Next look at Column 5 & 6 and determine which of those two columns has the most circles. That column number is your secondary number. Write the number in the box to the right.

Secondary Number

Column 5 means overall you're Passive, and 6 means you're direct in how you communicate.

Now use these two numbers to determine your Popular Personality Style.
If your *primary number is 1,* then your Character is **"Miss Priss"**.
If your *primary number is 2,* then your Character is **"Prom Queen"**.
If your *primary number is 3,* then your Character is **"Lady Diva"**.
If your *primary number is 4,* then your Character is **"Miss Perfect"**.

Your Style

Write your Personality Style in the box to the right and turn the page to read more about your Popular Personality highlights!

Popular Personality Type

STEP #2

Now That You've Identified Your Individual Personality Type, Turn The Page to Find Out What Character Highlights You Can Use To Enhance Your Image!

Your Character at a Glance, if you're a "Miss Priss"

Your Character at a Glance, if you're a *"Miss Priss"*

Miss Priss Ladies...

- Are considerate of others.
- Will meet the needs of others before their own.
- Are team players, and let others make decisions in a group setting.
- Are appreciative and like appreciation in return.
- Base relationships off their personal feelings.
- Tend to take things personal.
- Are trustworthy.
- Take time to make friends, but keep them for a lifetime.
- In conflict they discuss their personal feelings on the matter verses facts.
- Like to be listened to and like to listen to others.
- Are less likely to voice their opinions to avoid misunderstandings.
- Do not like a lot of attention. (very discreet)
- Are more of a "follower" than a "leader". (like to blend in with the crowd)
- Like to provide assurance and support.
- Tend to be shy or quiet at times.
- Tend to work with people they like in order to complete a task.
- Find it hard to work with or around people they don't get along with.
- Are very pleasant and friendly.
- Are reliable.

Why "Miss Priss" is Popular

Miss Priss ladies are considerate of people and will meet the needs of others before her own. She is appreciative and likes appreciation in return. *Miss Priss* bases her relationships off personal feelings and tends to take things personal. *Miss Priss* is trustworthy! When meeting people she takes her time to make friends, but keeps them for a lifetime. When conflict arises she discusses her personal feelings on the matter verses facts.

Miss Priss likes to be listened to and likes to listen to others in return. However, she is less likely to voice her opinions to avoid misunderstandings, and she does not like a lot of attention. *Miss Priss* considers herself more of a "follower" than a "leader" because her best qualities are helping people rather than "bossing" them around. Her strong points are that she likes to provide assurance and support to those around her, and she likes to create a friendly environment wherever she goes, which is why people love being around her!

Miss Priss tends to be shy or quiet, and tends to work with people she likes in order to complete a task. Sometimes she finds it hard to work with or around people that she doesn't get along with.

Overall, *Miss Priss* ladies are very elegant, and pleasant. They value being friendly, and are very reliable!

Your Character at a Glance, if you're a "Prom Queen"

"Prom Queen" ladies...

- They understand the importance of "attention to detail".

- Need specific information and details in order to make the right decision.

- Are thorough and take their time to think things through.

- They are accurate.

- Very organized and somewhat picky.

- Are skeptical and realistic about situations and people.

- They complete the job once and right the first time without having to go back and fix problems that were overlooked in the beginning. (most of the time)

- They are to the point and direct.

- They solve problems with "action", not just "talk".

- They listen and base their decisions on facts not rumors or assumptions.

- They are reliable and stick to getting the job done. They don't like people who do jobs half way or incomplete, or that don't keep their promises.

Why the "Prom Queen" is Popular

Prom Queens understand the importance of "attention to detail", and need specific information in order to complete tasks accurately. A *Prom Queen* is thorough and takes her time to think things through in order to make the right decision.

Prom Queens are accurate, very organized and have a high style of fashion and dress! She is to the point and direct, and solve problems with "action", not just "talk". She sticks to her promises and expects others not to break their promises. Though she hears gossip, she is wise enough to base her opinions on facts, and not rumors or assumptions.

Prom Queens are somewhat picky, and are skeptical and realistic about situations and people. A *Prom Queen* gives her best effort to complete the job once and right the first time without having to go back and fix problems that were overlooked in the beginning. She is reliable and sticks to getting the job done. *Prom Queens* are easily turned off by people who do jobs halfway or incomplete, or that don't keep their promises.

Above all, *Prom Queens* are the center of attention! They carry themselves with sophistication, class and confidence and are very understanding. A *Prom Queen* loves to solve problems without being involved in a lot of drama.

Your Character at a Glance, if you're a "Lady Diva"

Lady Divas are...

- Goal oriented and good at achieving goals. (perseverance)

- Like to be the leader in group settings.

- Base their success off of their accomplishments.

- Likes fashion, and usually sets the trend in popular fashion at school and work.

- Like to take control of the situation by themselves.

- Are open to new ideas and people but are opinionated.

- Find reasons to justify why their ideas sound better.

- Are fast paced and action oriented.

- Are business minded.

- Are precise, efficient and well organized.

- Are detail-oriented but want immediate solutions!

- Will debate facts not personal feelings.

- Are able to work with people they may not like in order to get the job done.

- Are direct and usually tell people "don't take it personal".

Why "Lady Diva" is Popular

Lady Diva likes to be in control of what's going on around her so that she is not caught off guard. She bases her success off of her accomplishments. *Lady Diva* is open to new ideas and people, BUT she can be opinionated in her speech, tone of voice and body language. She is fast paced and action-oriented and carries herself with style and professionalism. *Lady Diva* is very business minded and is classy in all settings. She is precise, efficient, well organized and is known for her good taste in fashion and style. She is detail-oriented and wants immediate solutions and results.

Lady Diva is goal-oriented and good at accomplishing her goals through dedication and perseverance. *Lady Diva's* voice is firm yet graceful in grammar and speech. Although she speaks in a direct manner, she is able to get her point across without being rude or offending people. She is able to work with people that she may not like, but will put her personal feelings aside in order to work together to get the job done. *Lady Divas* are direct and usually tell people "don't take it personal".

They like to share their ideas and are very creative and love creating new fashions and styles! *Lady Diva* loves to solve problems by talking, followed by immediate action and results, no delays. *Lady Diva* is not stuck on her titles, popularity, and recognition, BUT she does want a "thank you" every now and then.

Overall, *Lady Divas* are very classy and sophisticated with unlimited charisma and charm to get what they need accomplished in a timely manner. They value their reputation, appearance, and being "lady-like" at all times. *Lady Divas* have phenomenal style and value perfection!

Your Character at a Glance, if you're a "Miss Perfect"

"Miss Perfect" Ladies….

- Like to interact with people.

- Like to get involved and help out.

- Quick to make decisions to get the ball rolling to complete tasks.

- Love new adventures, challenges, and meeting people.

- Love to get credit and recognition.

- Tend to make decisions off what feels right, verses what is right.

- Love receiving gifts, awards, certificates and trophies for their hard work.

- Like completing tasks fast, even if they have to go back and re-do it after messing up the first time.

- Is upbeat, excited and carries an air of confidence.

- Is optimistic and finds the good in people and situations.

- Is open to new ideas and change.

- Bounces back quickly from disappointments and hurts.

- Doesn't dwell on negative issues for long periods of time, in order to move on.

- Solves problems by talking it out. They are talkers more than doers.

- Is very supportive.

- Love to compete.

Why "Miss Perfect" is Popular

Miss Perfect absolutely loves to interact with people. She likes to get involved and help out to make a difference in her community. *Miss Perfect* is quick to make decisions to get the ball rolling to complete tasks. She loves new adventures, challenges, and meeting people. *Miss Perfect* tends to make decisions based off what feels right, verses what is right. She loves receiving gifts, awards, certificates, trophies, credit and recognition for her deeds and her hard work.

Miss Perfect is usually upbeat, excited and carries an air of class and sophistication. She has an extremely high level of confidence and does not bother with what people say of her, because she values her self-worth and is not easily threaten by others.

Miss Perfect is very optimistic and finds the good in people and makes the best out of every situation. She is open to new ideas and change and bounces back quickly from disappointments and hurts. *Miss Perfect* doesn't dwell on negative issues for long periods of time, in order to move on. She solves problems by talking it out in a professional manner, without drawing negative attention. *Miss Perfect* is a talker more than a do-er, and has good speech and tone articulation. She likes completing tasks fast, even if she has to go back and re-do it after messing up the first time. She is very supportive, and loves to compete by taking part in many competitions including beauty pageants, sports, singing, playing an instrument, cooking, etc.

Overall, *Miss Perfect* answers to the call of duty to help her fellow neighbor. She is super-girl when it comes to supporting her family and friends and loves to live life. She is very dainty but doesn't mind rolling up her sleeves to work. She values creative fashion in a modest, elegant way.

Your Unique Etiquette Diary
STEP #3

To complete the last step, turn the page and start your final Blueprinting process to create your Etiquette Diary designed specifically for you, to enhance your popularity!

Turn to the following pages if you are:

If you're a "Miss Priss" Lady....

Below is your customized Etiquette plan. Turn to the pages listed below to learn, step by step, how to reshape your image. Practice this etiquette plan at least 3 times a week to increase your Popularity!

Quick Tips to Enhance Your Popularity

Be entertaining and fast pace. Support people's ideas and goals. Be ready for change and to try new things. Agree on the facts and remain optimistic and excited about the outcome or results. The best way to make more friends is to involve other people in activities like going to watch a game, going shopping or to the movies. If conflict arises and you disagree on a matter don't take it personal just debate the facts. Speak up and ask to take turns on group ideas and team projects, because your opinion matters too! Avoid being intimidated by people. Most of them are not out to make enemies, but do not spend a lot of time trying to make friends. Sometimes people may talk very blunt and direct but don't take it personal. Above All, always show people your good side.

If you're a "Prom Queen" Lady....

Below is your customized Etiquette plan. Turn to the pages listed below to learn, step by step, how to reshape your image. Practice this etiquette plan at least 3 times a week to increase your Popularity!

<u>Your Etiquette Diary</u>   Practice 3x a week | Completed

- Posture & Poise...page 21   _____
- Hand Etiquette...page 25   _____

- Facial Expressions...page 23   _____

- Use Your Natural Voice...page 42   _____

- Speech Courtesies & Delivery Tips...page 42   _____
- Beauty Queen Walk...page 22   _____

- Everyday Etiquette...page 52   _____
- When in Public...page 52   _____

Quick Tips to Enhance Your Popularity

Allow people time to get to know you. Show that you are "actively" listening and that you're interested about what they say. Ask them their opinions on ideas, tasks and topics. When you disagree, discuss personal matters before facts. Create a friendly environment for people to feel comfortable to get the task done. Support their feelings by showing support. Don't rush people, but allow them to move at their pace. Assure them that you are not out to get them. Be ready for change and to try new things. Agree on the facts and remain upbeat and excited about the outcome or results. Above all be genuinely interested in getting to know people.

If you're a "Lady Diva" Lady....

Below is your customized Etiquette plan. Turn to the pages listed below to learn, step by step, how to reshape your image. Practice this etiquette plan at least 3 times a week to increase your Popularity!

Your Etiquette Diary	Practice 3x a week	Completed
• Visual Poise: Fingers...page 27		_____
• Speech Courtesies & Delivery Tips...page 42		_____
• Beauty Queen Walk...page 22		_____
• Sitting with Style...Page 28		_____
• Don't Take it Personal...page 31		_____
• Body Discipline & Visual Poise...page 24		_____
• Everyday Etiquette...page 52		_____
• When in Public...page 52		_____

Quick Tips to Enhance Your Popularity

Use action to back up your words. Be exact, prepared and organized when working or studying. Always provide factual information when presenting ideas. Support others direct approach and try not to rush them. Avoid bringing assumptions to people but stick to the facts. Avoid getting upset if you don't win everyone's friendship and trust the first time you meet. Allow people time to get to know you. Always pay close attention to details and listen closely. Above all, let people see your excited and optimistic side.

If you're a "Miss Perfect" Lady....

Below is your customized Etiquette plan. Turn to the pages listed below to learn, step by step, how to reshape your image. Practice this etiquette plan at least 3 times a week to increase your Popularity!

Your Etiquette Diary	Practice 3x a week | Completed
• Beauty Queen Walk...page 22	_____
• Use Your Natural Voice...page 42	_____
• Facial Expressions...page 23	_____
• Body Discipline & Visual Poise...Page 24	_____
• Proper Greetings...page 43	_____
• Sitting with Style...page 28	_____
• Everyday Etiquette...page 52	_____
• When in Public...page 52	_____

Quick Tips to Enhance Your Popularity

Be precise, productive, and organized. If you disagree on a matter don't take it personal just debate the facts. Ask to take turns on group ideas and team projects. Be open to meeting new people and ideas. Don't be intimidated by people. Most of them are not out to make enemies, but do not spend a lot of time trying to make friends. Sometimes people may talk very blunt and direct but don't take it personal. If you make a promise, stick with it and act fast. Always remember to thank others that help you. Above all show people your good side at all times.

Chapter 2: Posture & Poise

You Are What You Think!

How many times were you told as a child to 'sit up straight', 'don't slouch', or to 'stand up tall'? There is a good reason for that. Body posture and poise allows a lady to carry herself flawless at any given moment. Many popular girls today have kept to the art of graceful poise because they know that image is everything!

Quick Start: In this section, Posture and Poise (also known as body-language), are small intricate details that have the ability to make or break your reputation.

Beauty Queen Walk

For popular girls, a confident walk is good posture in motion, and movement is what develops good poise. When a lady enters the room she wants to make an entrance, and walking is one of the most important details that enhances her identity. Your walk shows your sophistication and level of self-esteem.

For females, it is the slight movement in the hips that begin the motion for walking, not the foot or legs. The length of a lady's stride is determined by how tall she is and how long her legs are. (The average stride is about one foot for women).

Your Turn!

- Find a clear area to practice your walk. Ladies practice walking with low to medium heels.
- Minimize the space between your legs.
- Feet are turned out just the tiniest bit and placed in a straight line.
- Place one foot in front of the other. The average stride is about one foot for women.
- Keep your chin up and leveled. Shoulders back, and arm movement begins at the elbow.
- Walk straight out. Weight is not on heels, but on the inner pressure of the foot.
- Step lightly. With each step, your heel hits the ground first, and quickly rolls to the pressure point under the big toe.
- Try to glide across the floor. This shift of weight is done smoothly using your hips, with a continuous, fluid motion. (not too much bounce in hips)

Walking No-No's:

- Please do not bob up and down while walking.
- Try not to walk with your feet turned in [pigeon toes] or turned out.
- Do not lead with your head, or slouch while walking.
- Do not swing your hips, creating too much bounce.
- Try not to take really huge giant strides or tiny baby steps.
- Try not to swing your shoulders too much. Remember your arms and elbows create movement for your upper torso while walking.

Women's History Fact: For ladies, the traditional training method of the early 1900's was to practice walking with a book on their head. Balancing a small/medium book on top of your head forces your body into proper alignment – and that is the foundation of both good posture and an attractive walk!

Facial Expressions

The number #1 indicator of our mood is our facial expressions. Sometimes we may be in a good mood, but our face does not reflect it. Body language is very important when engaging in conversations with other people. As well, facial expressions will help you in picking up on other people's mood so that you know how to engage them in a conversation. Please know that not all facial expressions necessarily indicate how a person is actually feeling.

Eye Contact

It is believed that the most successful women in the world are those who rarely break eye contact with people they're interacting with. For people, being seen is being felt. People want to feel like they belong. When a lady maintains eye contact during a conversation it signals to those around her that she can be trusted, and is interested. Remember, eye contact is not the same as staring.

Tip: When talking to a group of people, steadily move your eyes from one person to the next with confidence and articulation.

Advantages

- When you make eye contact with people you will notice how they are more willing to open up to you, which will result in new friends and success at school, work and home.

Disadvantages

- Lack of eye contact will not make other's feel welcome or comfortable around you.
- Lack of eye contact could make you appear uninterested.
- Intense eye contact and/or seductive looks can lead to improper conduct and a negative reputation.

Body Discipline & Visual Poise

The way you position your body can send a clear message to people whether you are interested in them or not. Posture is the manifestation of attitude. Every pathway from the brain leads to a muscle. How you feel and what you're thinking about influences every move and muscle action you make throughout the day. In essence, you are what you think!

Your Turn!

To project a slim and taller image:

- Keep your head as straight as possible, and lift your chin slightly. This ensures that your back stays properly poised and eloquently lengthens your spine. Your eyes should move accordingly with your head. This projects a controlled and graceful manner.

Advantages

- If you are excited and sincere, people will feel the support and trust radiate from the expressions of your body language.

Disadvantages

- If your body language seems uninterested, people will think you are uninterested in them as well.

Posture No-No's:

- When a lady bends her head down or slouches, it makes her appear vulnerable.
- Appearing vulnerable could lead to people taking advantage of you.
- To avoid falling into uncomfortable peer pressure, always keep your head lifted at all times. This shows a level of self-confidence and self-control.

Hand Etiquette

Showing your hands is more attractive and appealing than hiding them. Hiding your hands is a fast way to sabotage your overall first impression. It suggests that you have something to hide, or that you're not telling the full truth.

Using your hands helps to balance your voice so that you're not overly aggressive, harsh or overly hyper with your words. Most people don't know what to do with their hands when they are in public. Here are some important hand tips to use.

Your Turn!

• Do not fidget/play with your nails, rings, hair, hands, etc. This takes away from what you're saying, and is very distracting to others.

• If your hands are free and not moving or gesturing, hold them by the level of your waist, slightly touching.

• Hands should be kept at your waist level in a relaxed position until you're ready to speak. Only then should your hands be used to emphasize a point.

• Hands should not be overused when conversing — it creates unintended distractions.

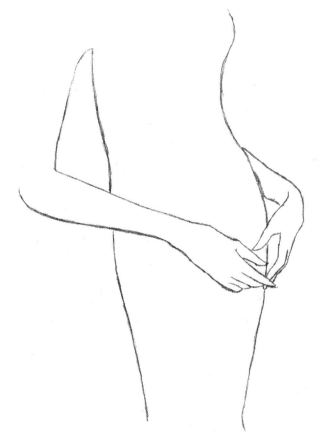

Handshakes: Your handshake says a lot about your level of confidence. It is polite to shake hands with the person[s] you are meeting. Keeping eye contact while you are shaking their hand is a great first impression. Here are tips when shaking hands in a professional setting.

• Offer a confident hand shake and greet the person using their name.
• As you're approaching someone, extend your right arm when you're about three feet away.
• Avoid shaking only the fingers or holding on to a person's hand after they let go of yours.

- Stand when shaking hands. If you're sitting behind a desk, stand up and come from around your desk to shake hands.
- Shake the other person's hand two to three times and let go.
- Shake hands at the beginning and ending of a conversation.

Visual Poise: Fingers

Fingers add tone and atmosphere to what you are saying with your hands. Fingers are very sensual and can be used to enhance your image as a sophisticated and feminine lady.

Your Turn!

- For example, when resting your chin on your hand, try not to ball your hand into a clenched fist. It conveys a message that you're aggressive or defensive.

- Instead, slightly open your hand and rest your chin on your fingers. By doing this you immediately soften your appearance.

- As well, whenever you reach for someone or something, your thumb and middle finger need to come together. Imagine that you are picking up a tissue when reaching with your middle finger and thumb.

Advantages

- You soften your appearance and appear interested in what other people are saying.

Disadvantages

- Balling your hands into a fist may appear like you are angry, aggressive or defensive.
- Resting your head into your open palm- in a slouched position- can convey that you are bored or tired.

Sitting with Style

For ladies, when sitting, the popular and elegant way for females to sit in all settings is listed below.

<u>Your Turn!</u>

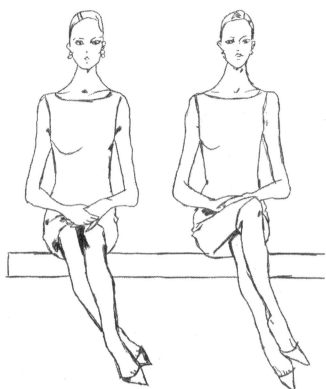

- Smooth the skirt/pants under you, and do not sit with your legs apart. Remember you are wearing a skirt and not jeans. And even when wearing pants, ladies sit with their legs crossed or close together.

- Sit straight down on a chair, and cross your legs at the ankles or just place the legs together with the heels slightly to the rear. Move them slightly to the left of you. This is known as the *Royal Family Pose*.

- Another proper sitting format is the *Traditional Leg Cross*, whereby you cross your legs at the knees and keep your legs tightly closed, with your ankles pressed in.

- Keep your back straight up, try not to lean against the back of the chair. If you do feel like leaning back, do not slouch in the chair, but sit erect.

- Rest your hands gracefully on your lap, by placing your right hand on top of your left hand.

<u>Posture No-No's:</u>

- Slouching and exaggerated stances- like the Military Stance- are the typical postures that can cause undue stress and fatigue to the back.

Chapter 3: Gossip Girls Etiquette

Proper etiquette is necessary for every lady. It's a must for every female with self-confidence, who recognizes the importance of being beautiful. In this section, etiquette is made up of more than just knowing which fork to use at the dinner table. Etiquette means you can maneuver through any situation with ease and assurance.

Quick Start: in this section, whether you're at an interview or on a dinner date, you will have confidence! And when you have confidence it not only makes you feel good, but it makes those around you feel important and respected.

Gossip Girls Etiquette

Gossip Girls are known for switching from one situation to the next without breaking a sweat. They have a level of confidence that is superb! Which is why they are able to talk to everybody in a friendly manner, thereby making friends everywhere they go. Hence, that's why they know EVERYBODY'S business!

This section will discuss the good traits of Gossip Girls, and will also point out the NOT so good traits of why gossiping can also ruin your popularity and overall reputation.

Gossip Girls Good Traits

Always Smile

Even when you are having a bad day, learn to smile. Most people you encounter for the first time don't know that you chipped a nail while falling down the stairs earlier that day, so try not to take your frustrations out on them. There's nothing like a smile to create a good first impression. Gossip Girls know that a warm and confident smile will put them and the other person at ease. This allows people to be comfortable in their presence. (which is why Gossip Girls have a lot of friends).

Be Courteous and Attentive

Gossip Girls know that First-Impressions Count! Good manners and polite, courteous behavior will help make a good first impression. Most of the time your attitude will show in everything you do. In fact, displaying a lack of manners can greatly ruin the one chance you have at making that first impression. So be your best, even when you may not be feeling 100% at your best.

It's good to remember people's birthdays, weddings and job promotions by sending flowers, congratulation cards and birthday gifts. Keep notes on people and important days that are special for them. A simple phone call or email to ensure people received your gift is a remarkable way to let people know that they matter. (which is why Gossip Girls are constantly on the phone talking to people).

On Stage Etiquette

The Golden Rule is to be polite to everyone and smile, regardless if they are not polite to you. Remember, you never know who is watching what you say or do, and how you treat others.

R-E-S-P-E-C-T

Try not to treat people according to how important you think their position or title is, or how popular they are in school. Treat EVERYONE with respect, even if they don't give it back to you. Gossip Girls get treated badly all the time for starting rumors, but they don't let that stop them from treating everybody nice. People you think are unimportant, i.e.-janitors or secretaries, actually have influential power to help or hinder your advancement at school, work and the community. Gossip Girls are good at observing how many people are involved in setting up meetings or scheduling appointments for the boss. Because it makes them more aware of how they talk to people and treat people.

Don't take it Personal

Address disagreements and conflict as "situation-related", rather than "person-related". Example, if your teammate forgets to turn in their part of the group presentation, you can express your disappointment about them not taking the assignment more seriously, instead of attacking their individual character and calling them names. Consider other people's feelings and stick to your convictions and beliefs as diplomatically as possible without imposing your views. Apologize when you offend other people. Address personal conflict off school grounds or outside and workplace, and find solutions to work it out.

Tip: Avoid raising your voice. Lowering your voice is more effective at getting people's attention than yelling.

Appreciation/Credit

Let EVERYONE who made a contribution or effort know how much you appreciate them. Speak well of their accomplishments. Avoid taking all the credit when other's contributed too, and avoid showing appreciation to a select few instead of everyone involved in the task. Regardless if you like them or not, still show people appreciation.

When receiving gifts, send a "thank you" note or phone call to let them know you received their gift.

Appropriate Dress for Ladies

Start with the way you dress. What is the appropriate dress for school, work or church event? In a business setting, what is the appropriate business attire? Should you wear jeans and a shirt or a skirt and blouse? The same for a formal event or formal dinner, should you wear a mini-skirt or a prom dress? And ask yourself what the person you'll be meeting or dining with is likely to wear. When in doubt, it's best to ask the coordinator of the event.

Be Conceited!

It's safe to look in a full length mirror at your personal grooming. Is your appearance tidy and clean for school, work or social occasion? A good hairstyle, clean and pressed clothes, and neatly applied make-up will guarantee you get noticed in the crowd and it will help make you feel more comfortable. If possible, carry a small pocket mirror in your purse to check your appearance. It's better if YOU see the food in your teeth first before your friends tell you about it in public.

Gossip Girls Bad Traits

Gossip Girls Talk Too Much

It is unattractive for ladies to gossip. Always speak nice of people. Remember, if you have nothing good to say, avoid saying it. When talking, speak on the facts and leave out personal opinions unless specifically asked to do so.

Avoid:

- **Intrusive Questions**- Unless they tell you, avoid asking questions like why they got a divorce? Or how much money they spent on their vacation? Until the relationship reaches a level of confidentiality, try not to engage in personal questions at the initial conversation.
- **Slang**- When in public, use words to ensure people around you understand what you're saying. When you're with friends it's okay to communicate in your own way.
- **Rumors**- Even if you know something negative on people, don't let them know that you know. Keep that to yourself.

Things that Sabotage Your Appearance

All it takes is just a few seconds for someone to evaluate you. Within one glance, the other person forms an opinion about you based on your appearance, how you're dressed, your body language, your mannerisms, how you walk, even the type of hairstyle you wear. These first impressions can be nearly impossible to reverse or undo. Your first encounters with people are extremely important because they set the tone for the type of relationships that follow.

Things that sabotage a good first impression:

- **Gum Chewing**- Many people chew gum to keep their breath fresh. However, gum chewing can be distracting and unprofessional at times. Especially when you're blowing bubbles or popping gum while someone is talking. Try switching to mints or candies, or chew gum silently.
- *Hygiene*- Being winkled, unshaven or smelly, whether it's the latest fashion or not, communicates to people that you don't care about how you present yourself, or who you're meeting.
- *Sloppy Language*- Society says that we are products of our environments. We find ourselves saying words we heard growing up, which may not be suitable for certain settings like the workplace, church or school. Make sure to use words that are correct in grammar and meaning. Practice looking up words in dictionaries.

- *Improper touching*- The only legitimate touching is the handshake. Hugs and pats are accepted in many countries, but vary in meaning and acceptance, so be careful.
- *Using lazy words* can hinder all of the hard work you put into your appearance and overall impression. Use words like "yes", instead of "huh" and "yeah". Use "Sir or Madam" instead of "hey" or "you".
- *Hiding your hands*- Etiquette research shows that showing your hands is more appealing than hiding them. Hiding your hands suggests that you're not telling the entire truth, or that you're hiding something.
- *Clearing your throat* too many times.
- *Giggling* too much.

Running Late or Forgot a Meeting

Regardless of how popular you are, all girls will have a time when they are late for an event. When this happens, offer your sincere apology without justifying your reason for being late. Making too big an issue of your lateness only magnifies the damage and makes the person more uncomfortable.

In the event that you forget a meeting or are running late, if the person you have an appointment with decides to cancel or postpone the meeting for another time, do not argue or pressure them to see you. Kindly request when they would like to reschedule the meeting. Let them reschedule the meeting on their terms and time, since you were late.

Interruptions

Offer apologies if you must interrupt a meeting, conversation, group project, or someone's concentration. If all possible avoid interruptions. If you must interrupt, kindly state the nature of why you interrupted and show consideration when doing so. Allow the person to respond on their terms and when they can get back to you. Avoid pressuring them to do something right then and there, since you did interrupt them.

Listen Up!

Most of your day is spent listening. It is very easy for people to get distracted from boredom, lack of interest or not fully understanding the topic being discussed. When people engage in a conversation, most of what is said is missed and forgotten, leaving only a small percentage of the conversation actually heard. This means that by the end of the day less than half of our listening skills are actually used. Below are ways to enhance your listening skills.

Tips to improve listening skills:

- Ask questions to clarify issues.
- Limit your own talking and try not to interrupt. It's hard to talk and listen at the same time.
- Paraphrase to validate or summarize what someone said, as a way of letting them know you were listening.
- Try not to stereotype or prejudge people when they talk.
- Avoid assumptions.
- Concentrate on important issues by asking questions and taking notes.

Chapter 4: Clothing Personality

Your *Clothing Personality* in this section demonstrates how you can create your own signature look that will be sophisticated, classy and timeless...and most importantly, Popular!

Quick Start: From casual weekends, to school activities, or a formal prom event, you will gain the confidence and style to go out into the world knowing you look...Simply Fabulous!

Clothing Personality

Your overall image through fashion and dress is another indicator of your popularity. Your clothes say a lot about your taste, your attitude, and your personality. When you dress clumsy and with little care, people will notice the clothes. When you dress with distinction and fashion and attention to detail, people don't just notice the clothes, they notice YOU!

Accentuating your wardrobe does not mean you have to spend more on clothes, but to maximize what is already in your closet.

It doesn't matter the clothes you wear but how you dress that matters. From the luxury fashion clothes to the local store clothing line, you can achieve a better look with the clothes you already have!

Fashion Trends

The fashion of Popular Girls is always well chosen with consideration of its purpose, and is always acceptable to the situation, whether it be school, church, work or a reception. When selecting fashionable clothes, Popular Girls will not permit their appearance and dress of the day to misrepresent their true integrity, poise and character. Therefore your clothes should always be fresh and clean and neatly pressed.

Wardrobe Management

Mix, match and multiply your garments and create several more combinations! Turn your existing wardrobe into a practical, coordinated haven. Start to view your closet as the investment it is, resulting in making smarter clothing choices. Wardrobe management will help you to organize your clothes based on your style!

Go into your closet and have a fashion show! Mix, match and multiply your garments and create several more combinations!

Pleasant Hygiene

The essence of a Popular Girl is in the intricate grooming of her day-to-day appearance. It's safe to look in a full length mirror at yourself. Grooming includes daily bathing, use of deodorant, tooth brushing, body perfumes and sprays. Having bad breath or body odor can be considered offensive. Make an effort to avoid this. Profuse (abundant) use of perfumes, especially when used to mask body odor, can be just as offensive in smell. Apply a little.

Colors

Color is the first thing people notice, so make sure you use it well. Color affects how we feel and how people will respond to us. Color is the essence of popular dressing. Wearing the right colors will define your physical features, give you confidence and create a positive first impression.

Advantages of wearing correct colors:

- You will be noticed immediately
- Your skin looks clearer and healthier
- Your eyes sparkle
- Your face appears more defined
- Your self-confidence is increased
- You will have people's attention. They are more likely to pay more attention to you.

Disadvantages of wearing too many colors:

- Bright colors can be tricky. Use them in small doses. Wear colors, but don't go too far that you are clowning around with your image.
- Color blocking can be distracting. Too many colors and designs worn together can be distracting to the eye and block people's attention of what you're trying to say. Choose 1 main pattern (Example- stripes or polka dots, not both).

What NOT to Wear...Ever!

The way a lady dresses affects how others view her. Many ladies are guilty of multiple fashion mishaps without realizing it, and sometimes her unsure judgment can lead to having a bad reputation, or being misjudged. Below are five tips on what NOT to wear ever!

Tip #1 Overdoing Fashion Trends

House shoes, spaghetti straps, tank-tops, pajama bottoms. Nothing makes a Popular Girl look less attractive than going to school or work like she is dressed for a slumber party or the beach. Having a "cover-up" garment nearby, like a jacket, will always make your outfit look more professional.

Tip #2 Too-Short Skirt

Wearing a mini skirt is acceptable. Wearing a *too-short* mini skirt may send the message (whether intentional or not intentional) that you're trying to give seductive intentions. Always remember that when you reveal your body parts, people's attention will be drawn to them instead of to your face. When you do wear a skirt, make sure you can sit down in your skirt without it showing too much thigh.

Tip #3 Too Much Cleavage

The number #1 fashion "No-No" for Popular Girls is showing too much cleavage. Successful women know that women who dress in sexy attire in public are more often passed over or not taken seriously, than women who dress more sophisticated and classy. When women dress too sexy or provocative, it sends an unclear message that they are more interested in getting a date, than they are in getting to know people.

Tip #4- *Wearing Men's Clothing*

One of the most discreet and silent taboos for Popular Girls is wearing men's clothing. Regardless if it's the latest fashion trend, wearing men's clothing will give the masculine appearance of a man, so avoid wearing it in public. School and work is not the time to show everyone your expressive lifestyle. Save self-expressive clothing for after school or work. Popular girls always give the appearance of being a lady everywhere they go.

Tip #5 Too Much Jewelry

One rule popular girls live by is: *Less is More.* Wearing jewelry can be confusing as when to wear it, how to wear it and how much to wear at one time. Costume jewelry can look tacky if worn in bulk. On the other hand, wearing real jewelry can sometimes come across as if one is "showing off" their possessions. A popular style includes one "show-off" piece of jewelry with subtle accessories, and visa versa. That means, if you plan to wear a chucky necklace, stick to minimal earrings and bracelets. Or, if you decide to wear your 24-karat gold bracelet, wear earrings and a necklace that are not as equally showy.

Feeling Overdressed

Many ladies have encountered times when they were overdressed for school, an interview or social event. However, they were able to regain their composure with ease and fit right in without causing negative reactions from the crowd. Here are tips on how Popular Girls overcome being overdressed.

If you feel overdressed:

- Don't panic or bring unnecessary attention in a crowd.
- If possible, discretely remove your blazer or jacket and drape it over your chair.
- Politely inform the interviewer, host, or the meeting coordinator that the casual dress code gives the place a warm, friendly atmosphere that you would like to be apart of.
- You're sending a polite message that you're not there to draw unnecessary attention away from the event.

Feeling Underdressed

For Popular Girls, it is sometimes harder to overcome being underdressed than being overdressed. However, they are able to maintain a sophisticated demeanor at all times. Here are tips on how to handle being underdressed.

If you feel underdressed:

- Don't panic or bring unnecessary attention in a crowd.
- Speak formally. Avoid using jargon, slang or colloquialisms ("you know", "totally").
- Mention that you were misinformed about the dress code and going forward you will dress more appropriately.
- Maintain elegance, and keep your posture poised and erect.
- Maintain a professional demeanor to substitute for your casual attire.

Chapter 5: Conversational Etiquette

A woman's voice represents the essence of her character. Conversational Etiquette identifies how you can make the most of your pure voice without feeling compelled to change your accent or natural tone. Learning the use of proper diction to fully express yourself will capture the full attention of your listeners.

Quick Start: In this section, Conversational Etiquette will allow you to control your natural voice in order to get your point across in the most eloquent and feminine way possible.

Talking

The art of conversation is a skill shared by popular girls, regardless if they are shy or like to talk. During a conversation, showing consideration and respect is just as important as receiving it. The art of conversation is a give and take between each person. Therefore one person should not be doing all the talking, and the other all of the listening. There should be a balance of expressing ideas and modest opinions.

Use Colorful Language

Remember to pay attention when people are talking to you and actively listen by nodding your head slightly or adding a comment in between sentences. Using words like "yes", or "that's great", lets the other person know you're listening to what they are saying, even if you're truly not interested in the topic being discussed. If you appear uninterested or bored you may hinder your chances of forming a relationship, gaining employment, and/or promotions at work.

Use Your Natural Voice

Always be yourself. Remain considerate to others who do not know you, as well as, those who may not easily understand your personality, choice of words and mannerism. Never be ashamed of your natural voice. Switching your voice to sound like someone else will make you appear false. Using your natural voice will make you appear truthful.

Slang

Using foul language and swearing will give "shock-value", and can be perceived as a lack of intelligence and eloquence in speech. This can lessen your chances of accomplishing the initial goal of the conversation and may offend people.

Always remember that without the ability to express yourself efficiently people can easily misinterpret your words and not "get" what you're saying. Present your best qualities at all times without losing your identity in the process.

Speech Courtesies & Delivery Tips

Remember to NEVER take for granted why we have forms of social courtesies and politeness. Saying "hello", "please", "excuse me", "thank you" and "how are you?" will advance you further in life than just skill and talent alone. You will notice positive results in the way other people perceive you when you demonstrate self-confidence and project a friendly image.

Verbal Conflicts

When you are verbally dealing with a difficult or sensitive situation, remember that the way you approach the person will determine their response toward you. If you are calm and soft-toned, then they will match your response. If you are aggressive, they will be defensive and aggressive as well.

Conversation No-No's

- Never criticize something or someone, regarding politics, religion, culture or race.
- Tell your positives but don't tell your negatives unless they ask.
- Keep your focus on the person you are meeting - give them the respect and attention you would like to receive.

Greetings- Make Your First 10 Words Count!

Try to start off your greetings with appreciation and thanks in the first 10 words of your initial conversation. Make sure to include their name. When addressing people use *"Sir, Ma'am or, Miss"*.

When responding, it is polite to answer *"Yes, Ma'am"* or *"No, Sir"* as a sign of respect-especially if the person is older than you, or carries a level of title, position and authority. It's okay to be causal when greeting your friends and social peers. The chart below gives examples on proper ways to greet people in a formal setting.

Formal Greetings

Introducing yourself	Introducing others	Responding
• **Good afternoon** Mr. Jones, it's a *pleasure to* meet you.	• Mr. Jones, *thank you* for taking the time to meet with us today. **May I** introduce my boss, Mr. Smith.	• *Pleased* to **meet you** Mr. Smith.

As with many forms of communication, greetings are cultural and may change within a culture depending on social status and relationship.

Small Talk

When you're standing next to a person and don't know what to say, small talk will always work. Small talk generally starts with social rules of polite greetings, courtesies, and inquiries about the well-being of others. Example: "Hi Mr. Wells, how are you doing today?"

"3-2-1 Action" Introductions

When you are introducing yourself to someone, the most important question to ask is "What am I doing this for"? Are you meeting someone to gain a job? To gain their support for a fundraiser? To meet new people in a city you recently moved to? Having a clear direction of why you are introducing yourself to another person or group of people will make it easier for you to speak and be yourself.

When introducing yourself in public, give the 3-2-1 Action Introduction! That means give 3 facts about yourself. Allow yourself 2 minutes or less to put your thoughts together. And give yourself 1 minute to speak.

See Susie's Example Below

1. I'm from California
2. I'm a Senior at Stone High School
3. I plan to major in Biology to become a Dentist.

"Hi Everyone, My name is Susie and I'm from California. I'm currently a senior at Stone High School and plan to attend college to major in Biology so that I can become a Dentist."

Write down 3 things about yourself [Your birthplace, hometown, school activities and groups you're involved in)

1._____

2._____

3._____

Now write a brief introduction about yourself.

_____

_____

_____

_____

Popular Girl's Etiquette
Cheat Sheet

If you are anxious to get started
right away, turn the page!
Even if all you do is read the Popular
Girls Etiquette Cheat Sheet, you
will see dramatic results in just
your first few days of reading this!
Then you can come back and use
the rest of the book to find out
what makes YOU Popular!

Popular Girl's Etiquette
Cheat Sheet

High School Beauty Secrets

In High School, fashion and appearance is an issue for many teenage girls. If you are stressing about what you should look like as an incoming freshmen or graduating senior, here's a quick guide to help you look more popular. [1]Read the following pages to discover your fashion, from 9th through 12th grade.

"Fabulous" Freshmen (9th Grade)

9th-Grader's should wear transparent (see through) glitter lip gloss, some mascara, and maybe a little bit of transparent eye shadow with a slight hint of glitter. Avoid going too heavy or it may look bad. If you want to try out more types of makeup, keep that for home experiments. Hairstyles should be simple, yet fashionable, like stylish ponytails.

As for clothes, keep them at a modest, fashionable level. Overall choose clothes that will make you feel comfort since you already have enough to deal with being a Freshman in high school. If you are wearing a bra or undershirt, don't let the straps hang out. It doesn't look cool, only sloppy. If you are wearing a short shirt, check in the mirror to see if your stomach hangs out of the bottom. Otherwise, wear something a little bit longer. This also applies to your skirts and shorts as well.

Remember to use simple accessories like jewelry and handbags [purses]. The point is to keep your makeup light, and your clothes clean cut.

---

1   *High School Beauty Secrets (9th-12th grade) is opinion-based and does not include medical suggestions for acne and other skin concerns. Please consult with your parents regarding acne/skin concerns, hair coloring, cutting and styles, certain clothing, and the amount of makeup to apply on.

"Sassy" Sophomore's (10th Grade)

In the 10th-Grade you are beginning to take a little more pride into what you look like. This year, you may want to start experimenting with different hairstyles (besides your typical ponytail). This includes letting your hair hang out with stylish curls a few days a week.

As for makeup follow the guide of your freshmen year, however you may start using eyeliners to enhance your eyes and facial features. Use pencil liners that compliment your eyes instead of making you look like a raccoon.

As for clothes, start matching outfits together with accessories. When you try out new things, make sure it looks good on you, not just in the picture or at the store. Find out what style suits you by shopping around in different stores.

"Sweet 16" Junior's (11ᵗʰ Grade)

In the 11ᵗʰ-Grade you are probably getting good at makeup and you know what you like. Add a natural foundation to your makeup. Start wearing soft color nail polish on your fingernails and toenails. When using foundation, first try it on weekends and ask your mother (or someone that uses foundation well) if it looks okay. Try establishing your own hairstyle without looking like everyone else. For example, if everyone has soft color highlights in their hair, try wearing your natural hair color with a layered look to add volume.

By now you're probably wearing tighter jeans and shirts and are probably concerned with impressing the guys, so it's safe to try out more mature styles such as a sleek skirt [not too high] and modestly low-cut necklines.

You should be wearing more than just tennis shoes. Try low to medium cut heels. If you are happy with your sports bra, that is totally OK. But it's safe now to go shopping with your mother or parental female adult to check out the actual bra department and wear something that makes you feel pretty - like lace.

"Sophisticated" Senior's

You did it! Graduation is upon you and you are trying to avoid "senioritis". This is a big transition as you prepare for college. By now, as you roam the halls of your school, you probably look like the rest of your peers. However, you should by now have your makeup and hair styles already. Try to update this look a bit, because no one wants to carry the same look they had in the 9th-Grade. Accentuate and dramatize your hair a bit more. Example, if you're known for parting your hair on the left side, part it even deeper, or switch to the right side. If you wear curls, make your curls even tighter or more loose. If you're wearing color highlights, change the color or go with your natural look. If you have a straight style, make it even hip and sleeker. The goal is to accentuate and dramatize your look.

As a senior you might want to wear your usual make up during the day, and as you start to go out with friends and boys at night, add a darker shade of eyeliner. Make your lips more festive with actual "lipstick" or non-transparent lip-gloss. It's also good to try new shoes, try wearing knee-high boots with a pair of hot jeans or a skirt and blouse. Try wearing open toe stilettos to show off your painted toe-nails. By now you should be painting your fingernails and toe-nails or going to the nail salon regularly for a pedicure and manicure.

Continue to add accessories into your outfit. It's time to switch your backpack for a suede or leather handbag to keep your schoolbooks in, this gives you a more mature look. As for your clothes and fashion, you know what you like, so go and find clothes that fit your style, but crank it up a notch for a more mature feel and look.

Popular Girl's Etiquette
Cheat Sheet
Fashion & Style

The public's perception of YOU is greatly influenced by what is seen. We have adopted a popular style of dress to help you project a glamorous image. This Fashion & Style quick sheet will have you looking sassy and sophisticated, polished, and poised. Overall you will have a pleasant attitude.

Popular Girls Secrets to Dressing Well

- Keeps clothing clean, pressed, and in fashionable condition (not too faded or torn).
- Keeps shoes clean and/or polished and in good repair (laces should be clean and properly tied).
- Matches accessories [i.e.-purse, earrings] to compliment her clothing selection.

Fragrance

- Use perfumes, body sprays and other fragrances sparingly (not too much).
- Dab perfumes behind the ear, the hollow of the neck and on the wrist.

Hands & Nails

- Hands and nails should be clean and neat at all times.
- Nails should be trimmed & polished at all times.
- Cuticles should be kept in well-catered condition.
- Nails are recommended to extend slightly over the fingertips or right at fingertips (not too long).
- Nails should not slow down the performance of your daily functions (i.e.-working, typing, etc).

Hair

- Hair should always be clean, dry and styled in a manner that is complementary to a professional image and a lady's features.

- Hair styles and colors should be conservative. Extreme styles and colors should be done with extra consideration.
- Bangs should be trimmed properly. It's recommended to be trimmed right above the eyebrow.
- Hair should not fall in or cover the face, but rather enhance and define your facial structures.

Skin & Face Complexion

- Complexion should be kept at its best with proper care, rest and diet. If commercial skin care products are ineffective, it is recommended that you consult a physician.

Popular Girl's Etiquette
Cheat Sheet

Everyday Etiquette

- Always say "please" or "thank you". No one likes a demanding or ungrateful person. When requesting an item, always say "please", and never say "gimme" or bark an equally rude order.
- Always keep your hygiene pleasant and complimentary to those around you.
- When making someone's acquaintance, it's always proper to shake the other person's hand and say "nice to meet you", or offer similar pleasantries.
- Cover your mouth when coughing and sneezing.
- It's never good manners to burp out loud, pass gas or show other rude bodily noises [like slurping loudly from your cup].
- Never interrupt when someone is speaking. Wait until you're sure they have finished before adding your own thoughts.

When in Public

- Consider the age of those around you. Some language or behavior may be inappropriate for other cultures, ages, and genders to witness.
- When standing in line, always wait your turn and never push those in front of you. Impatience is impolite. Remember, how you act to others, is how they will respond back to you.
- When visiting a movie theater, turn off cell phones, iPods, pagers and other noisy personal devices. Refrain from talking once the show begins and never kick the chair in front of you. You may even want to consider the subject matter of a film before buying a noisy container of popcorn or candy.
- Be sensitive to noise levels when talking, playing music or laughing.

Conclusion

Congratulations!

_____

(write your full name)

You have completed the Popular Girls Etiquette Diary Workbook. Through this manual you have gained a level of understanding on how to present yourself with a winning image. As a popular girl, you now know the importance of body language through visual poise and proper posture.

With your good manners, courteous behavior and positive attitudes you will be able to adapt to new ideas and new people, which will make a good first impression and gain positive results from others! With your formal and informal style of greeting you will form good friendships that will last a life time.

With your new style of wardrobe you are now able to mix, match and multiply your garment by wearing clothes that enhance your body contour, and accentuate your good taste in fashion. Your color selection reflects how you feel and how people will respond to you. Remember color is the essence of successful dressing. Wearing the right colors will define your physical features, give you confidence, and create a positive first impression!

Overall you have learned the intricate details of confidence and character that make Popular Girls Popular! After today, people will begin to notice a new you, including yourself!

You Define what Being Popular is!

_____   _____
Signature from a Witness (parent, friend, school teacher, etc)   Date

Additional books by Wilvena

Having traveled across the world, everything in these books has been tried and tested by the author, and that is what gives Wilvena the right to write such audacious work stating that every WOMAN is destined for success! For the stay-at-home mom, the corporate woman, the educated feminist, to the church-going diva, if you have the courage to read *"Miss Priss in the Office"* and *"Attributes of the Self"* and put these simple principles to work for you, you're *guaranteed* for *Success*!

Available at your local bookstores

- Attributes of the Self (2006)
- Miss Priss in the Office (2010)